Breaking
the Spirit of
Absalom

David Copeland

All Scripture quotations are taken from the King James Version of the Bible.

Breaking the Spirit of Absalom
ISBN 10: 0-88144-380-8
Copyright © 2009 by David Copeland

Published by
Thorncrown Publishing
A Division of Yorkshire Publishing Group
9731 East 54th Street
Tulsa, Oklahoma 74146
www.yorkshirepublishing.com

Introduction and Dedication

Many books, articles, and sermons have been written, preached, and taught concerning many of the most recognized spirits the church has had to contend with for the last two centuries. Jezebel, Python, Athaliah, and Delilah are just some of the spirits Scripture reveals who are at work in our midst in the 21st century church.

But in my own life, I have found an even more troubling spirit — one who has brought more defeat and hindrance to my life and assignment than Jezebel and Python: the spirit of Absalom.

I do not believe every negative thing we have to deal with in our lives is the result a demon spirit,. Some of the difficulties we face are because of unconfessed sin; others because of ignorance of God's Word. Still other problems are the result of generational curses and iniquity that is still operating in our lives. All of these things will bring hardships into our lives.

There **are** certain demon spirits assigned to steal, kill and destroy our lives. It is my prayer that as you read this book, your heart will be aware and your spirit alert to openings only you can close that satan is using to have access in your life. I pray that as you close these doors, you will find the liberty and freedom to experience and enjoy the next season God has scheduled for your life, free from the burden, guilt and oppression that Absalom brings to your table.

I do not claim to be a fantastic preacher, nor am I a stellar writer. Some things in my life I have learned the hard way, and some things I have learned by the Holy Ghost Who has set not only me free, but also thousands around the world where this message has been preached.

I dedicate this book to my wife Pam; to my daughter Megan and her husband Eric; and to Missy and her husband David; and to our grandchildren: Madison, Elijah and Andrew.

I also dedicate this book to my spiritual father and mother, Pastor Bobby and Joyce Powell. They believed in me and accepted me as their spiritual son when most people told them they were making a mistake. If I am anything good in this world, the blood of Jesus and grace of God are the first reason, and they are second! Their love, influence, and passion for the Full Gospel message has equipped me to be able to minister to pastors, leaders and congregations all over the world.

We see the story of Absalom's rebellion against his father, King David, in the book of 2 Samuel. In Chapter 18 of this book, beginning in Verse 9, the scripture reads:

And Absalom met the servants of David.

David has been chased away from Jerusalem by Absalom, who is now coming after him. David's chief military official, Joab, has been sent out to intercept Absalom. David is staying behind, sitting at the city gate wondering why this kind of trouble is happening again! Joab, Abishai, and Ittai have divided the fighting men who are defending David against Absalom's attack into three different companies. They are planning to ambush Absalom and take him out.

The story continues in Verse 9:

And Absalom rode upon a mule,…

Since this was before the days of the automobile, this donkey would have served as the royal limousine. Absalom did more than chase David from his home, he chased David out of his place of authority, away from his place of dominion and rulership. Absalom was using the things that were reserved for the king's use because he had usurped the authority of his father and declared himself to be king over Israel.

So as Absalom rode upon the royal mule, the story continues:

> ... and the mule went under the thick boughs of a great oak, and his head caught hold of the oak, and he was taken up between the heaven and the earth; and the mule that was under him went away.

I could preach right there! Taking what doesn't belong to you both spiritually and physically will leave you hanging in a predicament that could end your life!

Continuing with the story, we read in Verses 10-12,

> And a certain man saw it, and told Joab, and said, Behold, I saw Absalom hanged in an oak. And Joab said unto the man that told him, And, behold, thou sawest him, and why didst thou not smite him there to the ground? and I would have given thee ten shekels of silver, and a girdle. And the man said unto Joab, Though I should receive a thousand shekels of silver in mine hand, yet would I not put forth mine hand against the king's son: for in our hearing the king charged thee and Abishai and Ittai, saying, Beware that none touch the young man Absalom.

"Be gentle" is what David actually said — "Be gentle with Absalom for my sake." Verses 13-14 continue:

Otherwise I should have wrought falsehood against mine own life: for there is no matter hid from the king, and thou thyself wouldest have set thyself against me. Then said Joab, I may not tarry thus with thee. And he took three darts in his hand, and thrust them through the heart of Absalom, while he was yet alive in the midst of the oak.

Scripture reveals Absalom had a unique ability to grow hair at the fastest rate known to man. In fact, if you read the entire story of Absalom found in 2 Samuel, you'll see that he used to cut his hair every year and sell it in the marketplace. Tradition stated it became a lucrative business for Absalom. No one in all Israel had a head of hair like Absalom. It became his identity. But the very thing that distinguished him and set him apart from all of his other brethren, ended up being his downfall. Absalom's hair is symbolic of the pride and arrogance that had filled his heart.

As Absalom hangs in the tree, Joab kills him with three darts into the heart. See in Verse 15:

And ten young men that bare Joab's armor compassed about and smote Absalom, and slew him.

Our story concludes in Verses 16-18:

And Joab blew the trumpet, and the people returned from pursuing after Israel: for Joab held back the people. And they took Absalom, and cast him into a great pit in the wood, and laid a very great heap of stones upon him: and all Israel fled every one to his tent. Now Absalom in his lifetime had taken and reared up for himself a pillar, which is in the king's dale: for he said, I have no son to keep my name in remembrance: and he called the pillar after his own name: and it is called unto this day, Absalom's place.

In 2003, God spoke eight words to me that have totally transformed my life and ministry. I feel these eight words are important if we are going to understand the necessity of breaking the Absalom spirit. These eight words reveal why we are battling and where God is trying to take us in our life. God is calling, or more accurately, He is demanding that we get on with His program.

The first word is *transition*. The Church, the Body of Christ that is going forward with God, is in transition. Transition simply means change. Change is not a popular word with most church people. In fact, I can't help but think how the Church always seems to be 25 to 30 years behind everybody else in the world. I'm not advocating change just to be "changing." Contrary to popular political opinion, the only change you can believe in is the change that God the Father brings forth in our lives. But God is a moving God and He is working to change us more into HIS image. If you don't believe you are changing, get out your high school yearbook and find your picture. We are all going through changes. Transition is simply change or passage — passage from one place or stage to another.

As we go through transition or passage, we will be brought into a place of *reposition*. God is repositioning our mindsets and ministries in such a way that will bring us into a place and position of expansion.

Expansion, according to Webster's Dictionary, means territorial expansion. The territory of the kingdom of God is expanding. Most of the churches my wife and I minister in across the U.S. are in small rural areas. Many of these churches live in the shadow of a large congregation that seems to be growing by swallowing up the smaller congregations around them. Statistics show the Church in America is not growing because of new converts, it's growing by transfer growth. Many small churches and small church pastors feel like they cannot expand the kingdom of God because they don't have access to the same number of people and financial resources as bigger churches. Because our identity as ministers of the Gospel has been linked to how big our church or ministry is, pressure provokes these pastors to begin ministries and programs the Holy Spirit never told them to, all in an effort to compete with a bigger congregation somewhere! That pressure creates what I call an Absalom.

There are many little churches and small ministries led by pastors who have only been thought of as what my pastor used to call "little pecker-wood preachers." They'll never have a TV ministry; they'll never write a book or be listed as a "who's who" of their particular denomination. But they are faithful to do and work and serve where God has called them. Many powerfully anointed men and women who have been flying under the radar are about to be promoted by God! God is about to explode these faithful people onto the church scene with a message of healing, deliverance and victory! In the coming days, we are going to begin to hear about a lot of unknown pastors in insignificant places, of unheard of spots in America that are going to suddenly erupt in revival with an anointing that will cause them to become the new movers and the shakers in establishing the kingdom of God on this earth just like it's being done in heaven. Why? God wants all of us to enlarge our territory. Territorial expansion — taking territory away from Satan! Hell is enlarging itself daily, but may I remind you that heaven is also getting bigger daily too. And one single church in one single city cannot reap the national and world-wide harvest God wants to bring in.

Expansion leads us to *acceleration*. God is beginning to accelerate things for His people. People are going to get saved in the coming days and grow in God at such an accelerated pace, it's going to make some people who have served God their whole lives jealous! What used to take years to see happen in the kingdom of God will now take a month; what used to take months to receive an answer from God, will happen in a day. We have entered a time of acceleration.

As we allow God to accelerate His Kingdom plans in our lives He will bring us into *vindication*. While some will not be vindicated until we stand before Him on judgment day, others will be vindicated before then. Many reading this book need to be vindicated. God is going to vindicate your faith. If we will allow God to have His complete way in our lives, He is going to vindicate the decisions we have made that looked like

the silliest decisions a human being could make. But vin
tion will come because they were decisions made in the pra
closet hearing His voice.

Vindication will bring us to *validation*. The word "validate"
means to grant official sanction by marking. While the world
clamors recklessly for the mark of the beast, I want to have the
mark of God! This validation of God upon us will prove our
legitimacy which is birthed out of a heart of intimacy with Jesus.
Legitimacy can be defined as something born of lawfully
married parents. We are legitimate children of God. When we
leave this earth, God wants us to be able to leave a *legacy*, a
legacy that He has imparted to us. If Jesus should wait a thou-
sand years before He comes, He wants us to be able to pass a
legacy on to our children, to our grandchildren, to our great-
grandchildren that Jesus still saves, He still heals, He still deliv-
ers, He still baptizes in the Holy Ghost, and He's still coming
again! To God be the glory!

Before any of this can come to pass, before we can move on
with God's program, we must deal with and break what I call
the spirit of Absalom. God is commanding and demanding that
we deal with every sin and obstacle that would hinder our walk
with Him. He is commanding that we let go of everything. You
may say, "Brother David, I've let go of everything. I mean, I've
let everything go!" You will find, however, that the closer you
get to the Lord and the more Word you pour into your life, it is
inevitable that the Spirit of the Lord will reveal to you some
things in your life that may have been OK at one time, but they
are no longer OK. These are things that may not be blatant sin,

but they are things that have served their purpose. They brought you to this place where you are now but if you don't let them go, they will become a stumbling block, a distraction or even your downfall.

This applies to ministers, churches, evangelists, pastors, lay people...this is for everyone! Everything that we have accomplished while living on this earth will be judged in the light of His Word; including the motives of our heart. It's what we do in light of the Word of the Lord right now, which will bring the greatest joy to God's heart and the greatest fulfillment in our lives. Should we fail to walk in the Word He has given us right now, these things may bring our greatest sorrow and discouragement. God is calling us to break the power of Absalom in our life.

In my study on Absalom, I found that Absalom was the legitimate son of an illegitimate relationship. 2 Samuel 3:3, tells us that Absalom's mother's name was Maacah. In Hebrew, the word "maacah" literally means "oppression." David married this woman, a Syrian (Gentile) woman, during the years when he was running from King Saul. Everyone knew that David was destined to be the king over Israel. For him to take a wife who was not a Jewish woman and more specifically, to marry a woman who was not of the Israeli royal line, was simply opening the door for trouble in his life. A wife of David's either needed to be of the same tribe as he, the tribe of Judah, or she needed to be from Aaron and Moses' line, the Levitical line. By marrying a Syrian/Gentile woman whose name literally means "oppression", David opened the door for

Satan to kill and steal and destroy in his life. David created an illegitimate relationship and out of that illegitimate union was born a legitimate son. The relationship between David and Maacah was born out of frustration and fear during a time when David was running for his life. Absalom was a child of this relationship, born out of fear, frustration, anger, depression, and discouragement.

Everyone of us has given legitimate birth to things, ideas, programs, ministries, and problems that were the result of a relationship of frustration. We have all faced times in which we have become frustrated over a lack of God's moving and answering prayer; times in which Satan seems to be chasing us and our problems and insecurities are pressuring us to "make something happen" before we lose our church or ministry. Over a period of time, when the anointing begins to wane in our lives and ministries, instead of going back to God and the secret place of prayer and worship to recharge our spiritual batteries and renew God's vision for us, we begin to succumb to the pressure to buy into programs, ideas, and ministries that God never called us to be a part of! It's easier to buy into a program than to press into His Presence. It's at these moments that an unguarded heart will allow an Absalom to be conceived in your life!

David allowed himself to become involved in this relationship to begin with because of the loneliness he experienced and the persecution that came after he had simply done what King Saul had told him to do — go out and fight the battles for the nation. David was hired as the Chairman of the Joint Chiefs of

Staff, so to speak, and was asked to give his life to serve King Saul and the people of Israel. David was first obedient to God, and then obedient to the king and his leadership over him. Because of this obedience God granted David such military success that the young girls in the kingdom started making up songs about him. They sang, "David has slain his ten thousands but Saul has only slain his thousands." When Saul saw the blessing and favor that God had given to David and the success he had Saul's heart began to turn against David. David found himself running for his life from King Saul for 13 to 15 years.

Many in the body of Christ have gone through a season in which we have been frustrated and that frustration has provoked us to try to make something "spiritual" happen in the flesh. We have given birth to programs, we've given birth to ministries, we've concocted schemes and ideas and these may have been good for a time. They may have been wonderful and blessed a few people, but now, they are dead and dry and we are clamoring for some new program or idea that will get us over the hump into the next season of blessing. This Absalom you have birthed is rising up against you now in an attempt to drive you away from your place of spiritual authority.

Absalom will take our hunger and passion away. Absalom will tell you that the days of revival are over, that we're a bunch of lunatics gone in a ditch on the wrong side of the road. But let me assure you, the Spirit of the Lord is going to move and the glory of the Lord and the knowledge of the glory of the Lord is going to cover the earth as the waters cover the sea. My question is, are we going be among those through whom the glory of the Lord is flowing or are we only going be talking about when God moved "back then"? I choose to break the power of Absalom in my life and move forward with Jesus.

Every one of us has given legitimate birth to illegitimate relationships, programs and ideas in which God never told us to get involved. Until we break Absalom's authority in our lives, we will constantly be running after the next "hot" program to take our church or ministry to the next level, instead of going back to the prayer closet where our ministry was birthed to begin with!

Absalom was a vengeful person. In 2 Samuel 13, Absalom avenges his sister Tamar's rape at the hands of their older brother, Amnon by killing him. Amnon seduced and raped Tamar then drove her out of his presence in a fit of anger. In plotting his revenge, Absalom called all the brothers together for a picnic and before the picnic was over, he had killed Amnon.

Absalom was also insecure and afraid of being forgotten. We read in 2 Samuel 18:18, that Absalom raised up a monument in his own name. We are not here to raise up a monument to a denomination. We're not here to simply give honor to a preacher or personality. We're here to bring all the focus and all the attention and all the love and all the adoration back onto the only One Who matters — Jesus of Nazareth, the Son of the Living God. Oh, let us build a memorial to Him! If we're going memorialize anything or anyone, let us remember the things God has done in our lives and bring all of our focus on the works of God, not on what the hands of a man produce.

Absalom was also a deceiver and a seducer. 2 Samuel 15:6, says that Absalom stole the hearts of the men of Israel. While Absalom was stealing people's hearts, David was stealing the heart of God. Let me say this again: While Absalom was stealing the hearts of men, David was going after the heart of *God!* If Absalom were alive today, he'd sit in church and say, "Man, if I were only the pastor of this church…, if I were only the worship leader…, if they would only let me preach, bless God, I could do it like it's supposed to be done. If I could only be the king over this land…." If you have this attitude, it could be a sign that an Absalom spirit has its grip on your life.

There are certainly preachers who can preach better than I can. Probably every one of you reading this book can write or preach better than I. There will always be others who, according to some perspectives, can lead worship better, pastor better, administrate better — yet God has called us to do what only we can do. We are in our place or position because God called us there. God called us to be what we are, where we are.

Absalom would stand at the city gate and say, "Man, if I were king, I'd settle the conflicts. I'd take care of business. I wouldn't ignore people's problems; I would meet their needs! Where's the king? David's in the tent dancing before the Lord! He spends more time in that tent worshipping than administrating!" I believe David had this insatiable hunger just to worship; just to be in the presence of God. That blessed some people, but it irritated others. I think David understood that once you've been in the presence of God, you may decide to go back to stale religion if you want, but you're never going to be satisfied, you're never going to be content. You're never going to be completely fulfilled, because once you've been exposed to His presence; when you've been exposed to the deep cry of the Holy Ghost calling you closer to Jesus; when you've been stripped of a religious spirit and been caught up in a realm of the kabowd — the glory of God YOU CANNOT GO BACK TO CHURCH AS USUAL! Others have heard about this experience, they've read stories about it, they've seen it talked about in Charisma. They've seen it on TV, but when God supernaturally kisses and draws you out into a deeper intimacy with Him and His Presence, you will never be the same again! Once you've been called out by God, you may go and do other things, but if those things you are involved in are not mandated by the Holy Spirit, they will only create frustration. You can be involved in various programs and ministries and movements only to wake up one day to find that it's sapping the life right out of you.

At this time in Jewish history in which our story takes place, Solomon's elaborate temple had not been built. Moses' tabernacle had changed from what had originally been established. The sacrifices and special offerings were still performed at Moses' tabernacle in Bethel, but the Ark of the Covenant had been moved to Jerusalem by David early on in his administration. In the tent that David pitched in Jerusalem was the very emblem or piece of furniture that would forever bind the Jewish people to the Creator of the earth! Here was the Ark of the Covenant; that little box that told both Jew and Gentile that God was forever bound to these Hebrew people. The Ark of the Covenant was being housed in an open structure, exposed to the elements, not really receiving adequate protection. It was also exposed to every man and every woman, every boy and every girl who would want to get into the presence of God. While the Ark was covered and protected so you couldn't walk up and touch it, (people died in this day by touching the Ark — only the Levites were allowed to touch it) from all indications people were allowed to walk underneath the tent where it was housed. All they had to do was follow the king and wherever the king went, you could know that the presence of God was going to be there because David was a man after God's own heart. He had spent time in God's presence.

The relationship David engaged in that created Absalom actually started during those years when David was frustrated, when he was running for his life, when he didn't understand why he was living in the caves of En Gedi. During that time, he didn't have the Ark close by. He couldn't simply walk into the tent and talk with God. When you can't seem to get an answer from God or get close to His Presence to find direction for your life, it's then that you run the risk of creating an Absalom. When David was hiding in the back of that cave crying out, "God I don't understand why I'm running for my life? Why is Saul trying to kill me? All I have done is obey You and obey the commands of the king," Satan saw his opening. No doubt David had those moments in which he cried, "Why, why, why,

why, why?" And when the devil saw that opening, he made sure David found Maacah.

You don't have to go looking for oppression. Oppression has a way of looking for you. As long as we live, there will always be a devil. There's always going be a situation. There's always going to be a circumstance. There will always be somebody trying to keep you down, keep you under their thumb, keep you under their control. They don't mind you praising God, as long as you don't get too crazy. They don't mind you having revival as long as it stays neat and tidy. They don't mind you being exuberant in your worship, they don't even mind you wearing a little prayer shawl or doing a little jig every once in awhile. They don't mind you laying on the floor crying a few tears, just don't get all crazy and think it's what you're supposed to do 7 days a week, 24 hours a day.

It's not a sin to be oppressed, but it becomes sin when you allow that oppression to bind you and you begin to believe that's God's will for you. When you are searching for your identity in God and can't seem to find it, an Absalom will birth in your life. You can try to justify it by saying, "You know, God understands why I have this Absalom." Yes, God does understand where we are in our journey. Christ was a man of sorrows and acquainted with grief. But God is saying it's time to sever relationships with our Maacahs, it's time to cut ties with our Absaloms, and it's time to put away our alignment and our love affair with programs and ideas and ministries to which God never called us. It's time for us to put away our alignment with the oppressive religious programs that have drained the Life out of us and that have kept us from being what God has called us to be. It's time for us to submerge ourselves in the presence of God and know that God is going to raise us up to do a work in His kingdom in this hour.

Because David refused to deal with Absalom himself, Absalom chased David away from his place of dominion and he almost lost his throne forever. Friends, if we're going to fulfill the dream God has put in our hearts, we can't do it with people who are trying to oppress that dream and vision. It's been said that people who do not increase you will eventually decrease you. I'll go further to say that programs and ministries that are not given to you by the leadership of the Holy Spirit will only decrease you from your ultimate purpose. We cannot go forward in God with plans and programs and ministries that God never told us to do. We cannot carry any baggage into this next season in God.

I know from firsthand experience the problems having an Absalom in your life can cause. In 2000, I was offered an opportunity to purchase a broadcast license for a low power FM radio station to be located in Lanett, Alabama. It would end up being one of the first LPFM station to sign on in Alabama. I have always been a radio buff, going back to my early adult years of working in Christian radio when we lived in SE Tennessee. During this same time I began to sense there was a change coming in our life and ministry, and an increasing turmoil in the church we were pastoring at the time all added to the pressure to do "something" to find some kind of comfort and spiritual satisfaction. While the majority of the church loved us and took care of us, I became so oppressed and discouraged because I felt like the calling to travel and preach the Gospel and true ministerial fulfillment would never materialize. So I applied for the radio license.

In 2001, God released us from the pastoral ministry to travel as itinerant revivalists. After many months of frustrating delays, we finally received our construction permit in 2002, with only an 18 month window given to get the station on the air. Several restrictions were also placed in the construction permit that was basically making it almost impossible both physically as well as financially to put the station on the air. The biggest problem was we were too close to an existing AM station to put a tower up to broadcast from as that would interfere with the existing stations signal.

Through a series of miracles God miraculously gave us favor with the AM station owner and he advised us to put our antenna on his tower and the FCC would let us on the air. And it happened! On May 11, 2004 at 8:08pm, 7 days before the permit would expire, WRNK signed on the air with the song "Look What The Lord Has Done"!

But during this same time, our traveling ministry began to explode! We began having extended revival services that would last a couple of weeks at a time, keeping us away from home more and more; and at the station less and less.

All during this time, my wife Pam would tell me, "it's not God's will for you to have this station; it's taking you away from what He has called you to do!"

I didn't want to admit I had an Absalom! While there is absolutely nothing sinful about owning a 24 hour a day Christian Radio Station! It was blessing many people in the small coverage area we had! The problem was I had created this station out of frustration and fear of not accomplishing something significant for God with my life! and it became my Absalom. It began to suck the life right out of me! I knew what Pam was telling me was truth…even though I didn't want to admit it, I had created something while I was oppressed, discouraged and searching for an answer to bring comfort to my heart and fulfillment and validation to my ministry.

I knew if I didn't release this into someone else's hands, it would destroy me, the traveling ministry that I had waited so many years to be able to do, and it would destroy the radio station that was touching too many people just to permanently sign off! Finally on August 3, 2006, I turned WRNK over to another local ministry. I knew I had released my Absalom! Since that day, both Revival Now Ministries has experienced great favor and the blessings of God; and WRNK continues to gain favor and be mightily used my God, touching our local area with 24 hours a day- 7 days a week Praise and Worship music and the preaching of the Word!

What points can we take from the story of Absalom? *First, if we don't break with our Absaloms ourselves, God will send a Joab to do it.* When the Joab sent by God goes after our Absaloms, he will not show any mercy. I know this from personal experience because I've had so many Absaloms in my life that I have had to let go. In fact I couldn't just let them go, I had to drive them away from me. David was not willing to deal with Absalom. He wanted to coddle him, make excuses for him. His fatherly instincts told him to protect his seed. Absalom was a legitimate son, but he came from an illegitimate relationship. Don't misunderstand, I don't mean this in a carnal sense, I'm speaking of spiritual matters. We've created mindsets, understandings, and belief systems that we thought were Biblical, but they have absolutely no Biblical basis whatsoever. We've created ministries and programs and involved ourselves in projects with and for our churches that God never intended. We did these things out of frustration and burn out; out of a need to be validated; out of a need to be accepted and acknowledged. Now we wonder why there is no life, no joy, and why the ministry we are serving is really no better off than we were to begin with!

I am a revivalist. There's a lot of argument over whether God is finished with revival in America. One of the major "prophets" in America recently released a word saying there will never be another nationwide revival in America. There are many people convinced God is finished with America altogether — but not me! Because of the oppression, uncertainty, and fear that is prevailing at this hour, many are giving birth to an Absalom that says the days of God moving in power are over!

The line is being drawn in the spiritual sand, an even clearer, distinct marking between those who really want to go forward in God and those who only want to play the religious church game. These are people that can be identified by their attitude, their facial expressions, their giving and their taking, it is obvious that they have a life filled with Absaloms! These

people are really just takers, they're not givers and I'm not refer-
ring to money, either. They're always taking, taking, taking
from God, taking from the Church, taking from the praise and
worship, taking from the anointing. They want all the prayer,
they want all the recognition, they want all the pats on the back
but they do not really want to follow after God. They don't
really want the glory of God, the recognition of God, and the
presence of God to settle on a ministry like those who have the
heart of David.

David loved Absalom — he was his own son, third in line
for the throne. We love our churches and our ministries. If we
didn't, we wouldn't stay in them. But David needed to deal
with Absalom and we must deal with our Absaloms as well!
I'm convinced that if David had intervened earlier with his son
and helped Absalom break with the issues in his life, it's very
possible Absalom could have rightfully ascended to the throne.
But because Absalom's heart was wrong from the beginning
and never corrected, it eventually led to his downfall.

There are some people who will never fit in your life
because they would become an Absalom, they would become a
taker, they would become a destroyer, they would become a
seducer in your life — they would seduce you away from God.
They would deceive you away from God, they would draw you
into a place of compromise. Remember, the spirit of Absalom
doesn't mind you being spiritual or even going after God. It's
only when you go after Him with all your heart that the
Absaloms you have created in your life will rise up against you.
They will distract you. They will sap the life and joy of ministry

out of you! Because Absalom was born in oppression, out of a relationship created from oppression. The Absalom spirit only knows how to operate in and by oppression.

In reality, the spirit of Absalom is the male version of Jezebel, insecure and vindictive. This spirit invokes thoughts like, *It's got to be my way...we're the only ministry and I'm the only preacher doing it right...I'm the only, I'm the only, I, I, I, me, me, me!*

Because David was not willing to deal with Absalom, God had to send Joab to do the deed that David would not. As you read this book, you may have kids or know someone who has kids who are away from God and living their lives in total rebellion to what they were taught. You've done what was right in the eyes of God to bring your child up in the ways of the Lord. You may identify with David and be tempted as he was to overlooked the danger of Absalom saying, "Oh, he's my boy, be gentle with him for my sake." David's failure to deal with Absalom necessitated God sending Joab to do the work. Mark my words, if you don't close every door that has allowed Absalom to gain access in you life, the spirit of Absalom will drive you away from the presence of God.

The paradox of this story is that it was Joab who convinced David to let Absalom come back home after he fled following the murder of his brother, Amnon. When I speak of God's use of Joab, please don't think I'm condoning him because in reality, Joab was a wicked man. He was a blood thirsty warrior who looked out for his own interests. This story shows that

God will allow even a blood thirsty warrior to get into your life and remove whatever He desires, if that is what it takes to get your life back on track with Him. He will release the spirit of Joab to cut away those things that will stop you from being what He intends for you to be — the king and priest and ruler over your household, over your circumstances, over your finances, over your health, over your strength, over wherever the sole of your feet tread!

The second point we can see is that *God also raised up Joab to snap David out of his victim mentality.* In the early part of 2 Samuel 19, King David had his face covered up crying, "Absalom, Absalom, Absalom!" I'm not diminishing the fact that David had lost his son. It is only natural that a genuine father would mourn the loss of a son. At this time, David's whole world seems to have fallen apart — he'd lost his wives, he'd lost his concubines, he'd lost his home. He'd lost access to the presence of God and the Ark of the Covenant. The root of all this loss can be traced back to that period of time when loneliness aligned him with a wrong relationship.

David had created habits that would birth relationships that would hurt him in the long run. The habits you create determine the future you produce. Every one of us have created ideas, mindsets, ministries, programs and a structure of what we think church and ministry should be. But were those ideas born of the Holy Spirit? Do they align with the Word of God? Or do they exist because of a pressure or drive to succeed in the eyes of the world? Do these things exist because our denomination tells us this is what ministry should look like, or were they born of the Holy Spirit?

The older you get, the harder it is to discipline your mind, to discipline your eyes, to discipline your thoughts, to stay focused. Maybe you're having trouble staying focused right now. Because David was not willing to stay focused on pursuing Him by dealing with Absalom, God sent Joab to do it. God used Joab to snap David out of his victim mentality and out of his oppression. 2 Samuel 19:5-7 reads:

And Joab came into the house to the king, and said, Thou hast shamed this day the faces of all thy servants, which this day have saved thy life, and the lives of thy sons and of thy daughters, and the lives of thy wives, and the lives of thy concubines; In that thou lovest thine enemies, and hatest thy friends. For thou hast declared this day, that thou regardest neither princes nor servants: for this day I perceive, that if Absalom had lived, and all we had died this day, then it had pleased thee well. Now therefore arise, go forth, and speak comfortably unto thy servants: for I swear by the LORD, if thou go not forth, there will not tarry one with thee this night: and that will be worse unto thee than all the evil that befell thee from thy youth until now.

God has not called you to be overrun, He has called you to run over. God has not called you to be a victim, He's called you to be the victor, the overcomer. If you read the book of Revelation you'll see over and over and over, that the Word of the Lord speaks of "he that overcometh" or "he that over-comes." Really, the book of Revelation is about he and she who overcomes! God has called the Church to be dominion people! We've heard the message of dominion, we've heard the teaching of dominion, shouted about the message of domin-ion, but yet we've never been able to live it! I know about the teaching on dominion years ago called the Latter Rain. I know that some of the message strayed into false doctrine and birthed many unscriptural ideas in the Spirit filled community, but the truth still is that God has ordained the Church to be the head and not the tail. He has called us to be above and not beneath; lenders and not borrowers. We are not to take our cues from Madison Avenue or Hollywood. We accomplish His purpose by being baptized with a baptism of love, and by doing away with every Absalom in our lives.

Because we have linked ourselves with oppression, we have accepted what is called an unloving spirit. The unloving spirit thrives on a victim mentality. Some have walked through so much oppression in their lives, they feel guilty if they're not just a little bit depressed or oppressed! I've personally dealt with depression, I'm not making fun of it. I know depression is a demonic spirit from hell and it will make you do things and say things and act in ways that are not reflec-tive of the real you. Depression will make you believe things that are totally unscriptural. When you believe these things, you create an Absalom that later on, will try to drive you from your place of dominion.

God not only sent Joab to take Absalom out, but He also sent Joab to snap David out of his fog and say, "You are the king. You are the man after God's own heart. You are the one who danced naked before the presence of the Lord and lived to tell. You are the man that Messiah will come through! You are the only one besides the Levites, besides the sons of Obed Edom, besides the sons of Aaron who has been able to get close to the presence of the Lord and live to tell about it. Sir, you are God's man! You are a king! You are called to rule!"

The Absaloms we've created must be dealt with because they have distracted us from our assignment. We have failed to distinguish the difference between our task and our assignment. My task is to preach, to pray, to go to Guyana and do missions work in Kenya. Your task may be to work in Children's Church. Your task may be to be on the praise team. Your task may be to serve as an intercessor. Your task may be to be a psalmist or a songwriter. Your task may be to work in the prisons. Your task may be to work in the sound booth or to be an usher. But your assignment is to be in His presence. We've become confused on this point. That confusion is the reason why, when the Holy Ghost has moved in special, distinct ways as He has in many churches across the U.S., when that move begins to wane, we start grasping for a program that will bring the next "wave" of God's Presence. What we need to be about is getting back to what we're called to do. The Church began on the day of Pentecost with revival fire falling on the heads of 120 people and with tongues on fire, speaking the wonderful works of God! Jesus is not coming back after a Church that is any less on fire!

We're called to be intimate with the Lord. Once we have become intimate with the Lord, we're not going to give birth to an Ishmael or an Absalom, we're going to give birth to the Isaac.

I want to beg you in Jesus' name, your assignment is not to be like every other church in your town. You are not called to have another program like every other church; your assignment is to know Him. Your assignment is to be intimate with Him. Your assignment is to get as close to Him as you possibly can and then when He allows you to leave that place of your assignment, you'll be able to go out and do your task in a way that will not be frustrating; it will not be oppressive; it will not cause you heartache or pain. Even in the midst of persecution or destruction or problems, you will find the joy of the Lord and the peace of God that passes all understanding.

I have given birth to so many ideas and strategies that were really born out of oppression, grasping for something that would work, something that would take the ministry to the next level. These Absaloms I created almost drove me away from my assignment, and that is intimacy with God. I wish I had time to tell of all the Absaloms I've had to let go of just in the past year alone! But I can tell you that when I let them go, the peace it brought was coupled with joy unspeakable and full of glory.

If you are reading this book and you admit that there are some Absaloms in your life, I urge you to just let them go in

Jesus' name. For some, it may be may be a ministry that you're trying to make happen or prop up and keep going to which God never called you. For some, it may be an idea or a mindset that God's is calling you to let go of as you transition with Him into your next season. God wants to empower you to say no to the flesh! He wants you to begin to say no to the devil. There are some ministers reading this to whom God is saying, "Give your ministry to Me and allow Me to do the promotion. Allow Me to give you the programs I want you to have." Come out of discouragement or oppression or depression in Jesus' name. God has not changed His mind about what He wants to do in your life, through your life, and even to your life. If God didn't trust you to do what is right, He never would have called you to begin with!

Break the Absalom Spirit....today!

About the Author

David Copeland was called to ministry at 16 years of age. He served in pastoral ministry over 23 years in his current home town of Lanett Alabama.

Since 2001 David and his wife Pam have traveled across the United States and around the world conducting revival meetings, crusades, Pastors seminars as well as regular Sunday services. His years of service in pastoral ministry has equipped him with a burden and a passion to help pastors and their congregations experience a fresh touch of revival fire. Not just another series of manipulated services, but a genuine fresh touch of the Presence of God!

David currently ministers extensively across the United States in Sunday services and extended meetings and conducts regular trips to Kenya East Africa and Guyana South America. He has also ministered in Mexico, Trinidad, Indonesia and Nigeria.

David and Pam have been happily married since 1980 and have two daughters, two sons in law and the four most beautiful grandchildren in the world!

David also serves as director of Revival International, a network of ministers, ministries and churches that have a heart to see revival come to their local community. Revival International also equips, encourages and empowers men and women to do the Full Gospel ministry who are not able to gain acceptance in other ministerial fellowships.

Notes

Notes

Notes

Notes

Notes

Notes

Notes

Notes

Notes

Notes

Notes

Notes

Notes

Notes

CPSIA information can be obtained at www.ICGtesting.com
Printed in the USA
BVOW06s1316040915

416651BV00005B/15/P